D1118071

ARCHIVAL PRINCIPLES AND PRACTICE

A GUIDE FOR
ARCHIVES MANAGEMENT
BY

JEANETTE WHITE FORD

McFarland & Company, Inc., Publishers
Jefferson, North Carolina, and London

British Library Cataloguing-in-Publication data are available

Library of Congress Cataloguing-in-Publication Data

Ford, Jeanette White, 1929–
    Archival principles and practice : a guide for archives management
/ by Jeanette White Ford.
      p. cm.
    Includes bibliographical references.
    ISBN 0-89950-480-9 (55# alk. paper; sewn softcover) ∞
    1. Archives — Administration. I. Title.
CD950.F67 1990
025.17'14 — dc20   89-49030
                                          CIP

Manufactured in the United States of America

McFarland & Company, Inc., Publishers
Box 611, Jefferson, North Carolina 28640

TABLE OF CONTENTS

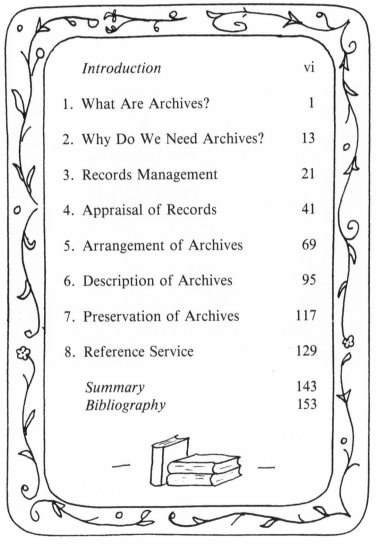

INTRODUCTION

... Musty books ... dusty boxes ... fading blueprints ... documents in disarray, a mysterious storage area inherited from "those who were here before our time."

These terms describe an area in almost every library, school, church, business or home.

"How can I bring order to this impossible collection?" you ask yourself. "Will I discover something worthwhile?" "Will I discard something of value?" "Where can I find guidelines simple enough to be followed immediately, but detailed enough to allow completion of the task?"

This book answers these questions. You can use it yourself or place it in the hands of volunteer helpers. The book can also be used by students who plan to pursue the study of archival principles and practice.

Although the tone of the book is light, the intent is serious — to equip you to establish and maintain your archives.

Jeanette White Ford
Ridgway, Colorado

CHAPTER 1

WHAT
ARE
ARCHIVES ?

ARE ARCHIVES

PLACES WHERE

HISTORICAL DOCUMENTS
ARE KEPT ?

THAT'S
RIGHT !

ARCHIVES ARE PLACES OR INSTITUTIONS WHERE NON-CURRENT RECORDS ARE STORED.

BUT, THEY ARE MORE THAN PLACES.

ARCHIVES ARE

ALSO CERTAIN <u>KINDS</u>

OF RECORDS.

5

NOTE THE THREE
MAIN WORDS IN JENKINSON'S
DEFINITION :

1. DOCUMENTS

2. OFFICIAL

3. PRESERVED.

1. ARCHIVES ARE DOCUMENTS.

DOCUMENTS CAN BE MADE
OF PAPER, WOOD, STONE,
TAPE OR ANY OTHER
MATERIAL WHICH CAN
CARRY A MESSAGE.

2. ARCHIVES ARE
OFFICIAL.

THEY WERE CREATED
TO KEEP ACCOUNT OF
TRANSACTIONS IN THE
REGULAR COURSE OF
BUSINESS.

AND, BY THE WAY...
HERE'S ANOTHER IMPORTANT
FACT ABOUT ARCHIVES.

ARCHIVES ARE
USUALLY THE
OFFICIAL RECORDS
OF A
SINGLE
INSTITUTION. ✭

✭ SOME ARCHIVES INCLUDE
SPECIAL COLLECTIONS, SUCH
AS PERSONAL PAPERS OR
MANUSCRIPTS.

GENERALLY, HOWEVER, AN
ARCHIVES COLLECTS ONLY THE
PERMANENT RECORDS OF A
     PARENT INSTITUTION.

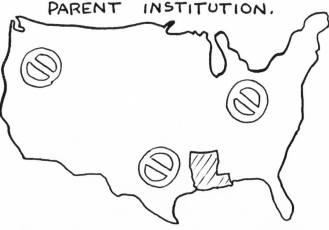

FOR EXAMPLE, THE LOUISIANA
STATE ARCHIVES ACCEPTS RECORDS
ONLY FROM THE LOUISIANA STATE
GOV'T. —NOT OREGON, OHIO, NOR TEXAS.

SOUTHERN BAPTIST SEMINARY
DOES NOT COLLECT RECORDS FROM
NOTRE DAME UNIVERSITY.

THE NATIONAL ARCHIVES
COLLECTS RECORDS CREATED
BY FEDERAL AGENCIES.

LET'S REVIEW.

Q. WHAT ARE ARCHIVES ?

ARCHIVES ARE P_____
WHERE HISTORICAL DOCUMENTS ARE
KEPT.

ARCHIVES ARE ALSO CERTAIN
KINDS OF RECORDS.

SIR HILARY JENKINSON SAID,
"ARCHIVES ARE D_____ DRAWN
UP IN AN O_____
TRANSACTION AND P_____
FOR INFORMATION.

ARCHIVES ARE USUALLY THE
RECORDS OF A S_____
INSTITUTION.

ANSWERS: PLACES, DOCUMENTS, OFFICIAL, PRESERVED, SINGLE

12

CHAPTER 2

WHY

DO WE NEED

ARCHIVES ?

HERE ARE SIX REASONS:

I. ARCHIVES PRESERVE PRIMARY SOURCES.

UNLIKE HISTORY BOOKS OR NEWSPAPERS, ARCHIVES ARE UNBIASED BY AUTHORS OR JOURNALISTS.

2. ARCHIVES MAKE EFFICIENT RESEARCH POSSIBLE.

IN AN ARCHIVAL REPOSITORY A RESEARCHER CAN HAVE A LOT OF INFORMATION AT HIS FINGERTIPS.

3. ARCHIVES PRESERVE OUR CULTURAL HERITAGE.

4. ARCHIVES FILL AN OFFICIAL NEED.

"IF WE COULD FIND THE BLUEPRINTS, WE WOULD KNOW IF OUR SCHOOL BUILDING FOUNDATION IS STRONG ENOUGH TO SUPPORT ANOTHER STORY."

5. ARCHIVES PROTECT THE PUBLIC INTEREST.

6. ARCHIVES FREE OFFICE SPACE FOR CURRENT OPERATIONS.

REVIEW

Q. WHY DO WE NEED ARCHIVES?

A. 1. ARCHIVES PRESERVE _____ _____ .

2. ARCHIVES MAKE _____ _____ POSSIBLE.

3. ARCHIVES PRESERVE OUR _____ _____ .

4. ARCHIVES FILL AN _____ _____ .

5. ARCHIVES PROTECT THE _____ _____ .

6. ARCHIVES FREE _____ _____ FOR CURRENT OPERATIONS.

1. PRIMARY SOURCES 2. EFFICIENT RESEARCH 3. CULTURAL HERITAGE 4. OFFICIAL NEED 5. PUBLIC INTEREST 6. OFFICE SPACE.

Chapter 3
RECORDS MANAGEMENT

WHY SHOULD
AN ARCHIVIST
CARE ABOUT
RECORDS MANAGEMENT ?

BECAUSE
  THE QUALITY
OF ARCHIVES IS DEPENDENT ON
THE KINDS OF RECORDS
  PRODUCED BY
AN ORGANIZATION.

BOTH ARCHIVISTS
AND
RECORDS MANAGERS
ARE CONCERNED WITH
THE WHOLE LIFE SPAN
OF RECORDS:

- CREATION
- MANAGEMENT
- DISPOSITION.

WHAT ARE THE

GOALS

OF

RECORDS MANAGEMENT?

THEY ARE ALMOST THE SAME
AS THE GOALS OF
AN ARCHIVIST.

THE GOALS OF RECORDS MANAGEMENT ARE:

1. CONTROLLED <u>CREATION</u> OF RECORDS.
   A. ADEQUATE DOCUMENTATION.
   B. PREVENTION OF UNNECESSARY DOCUMENTATION.

2. EFFICIENT <u>MANAGEMENT</u> OF RECORDS.
   A. EFFICIENT ARRANGEMENT OF FILES.
   B. ADEQUATE STORAGE.

3. PROPER <u>DISPOSITION</u> OF RECORDS.
   A. SYSTEMATIC DISPOSAL.
   B. PRESERVATION OF PERMANENTLY VALUABLE RECORDS.

NOW, LET'S LOOK AT THESE GOALS ONE BY ONE.

GOAL 1. CONTROLLED CREATION OF RECORDS

A. GOOD MANAGEMENT REQUIRES ADEQUATE DOCUMENTATION.

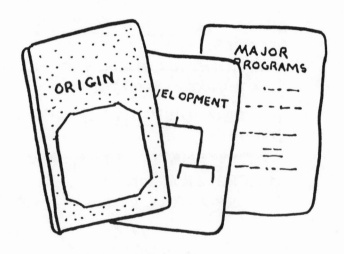

THE MOST VALUABLE RECORDS OF AN ORGANIZATION RELATE TO ORIGIN, DEVELOPMENTS, AND MAJOR PROGRAMS.
SUCH RECORDS SHOULD BE PRESERVED.

UNFORTUNATELY, MANY IMPORTANT DECISIONS ARE MADE ORALLY.

THE TELEPHONE IS "THE THIEF OF HISTORY."

LETTERS, FORMS, REPORTS, AND DIRECTIVES MAKE UP THE BULK OF DOCUMENTATION.

LETTERS

Shorten letters. ✔

Use pattern letters. ✔

Use form letters. ✔

FORMS

Forms should fit procedure and not vice versa.

Printed lines on forms should match typewriter spacing.

REPORTS

May be narrative or statistical.

May be a compilation of forms.

Some may be unnecessary.

DIRECTIVES

Memos, bulletins, and notices are usually temporary and may be issued in temporary form.

Orders, rules, and regulations are more permanent and may be issued in handbooks or manuals.

B. GOOD MANAGEMENT
REQUIRES PREVENTION OF
UNNECESSARY
DOCUMENTATION .

WITH THE DEVELOPMENT OF THE
TYPEWRITER
PAPERWORK BEGAN TO
INCREASE .   LATER,
CARBON PAPER MADE
MULTIPLE COPIES
POSSIBLE.

PHOTOCOPIERS

MULTIPLIED THE
PRODUCTION AND THE
PROBLEM.

FOR EXAMPLE,

EACH YEAR GOVERNMENT
RECORDS WOULD FILL A
FILE DRAWER ABOUT

1838

MILES LONG.

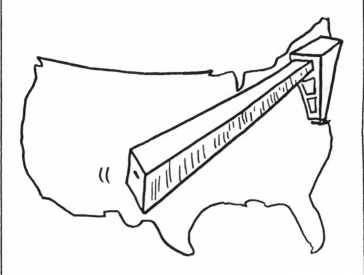

— THE DISTANCE
FROM WASHINGTON TO
ALBUQUERQUE!

OF COURSE,

ADMINISTRATORS

WANT

REPORTS!

EACH ADMINISTRATIVE OFFICE
WANTS ONE OR TWO "SIMPLE"
REPORTS.

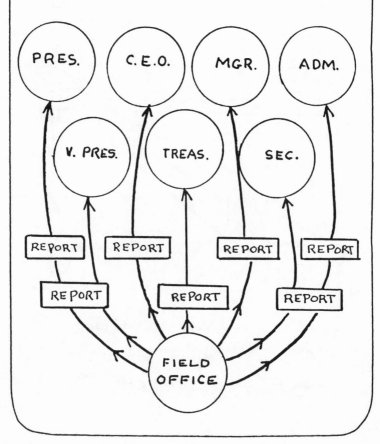

GOAL 2. EFFICIENT MANAGEMENT OF RECORDS.

A. GOOD MANAGEMENT
REQUIRES EFFICIENT ARRANGEMENT
OF FILES.

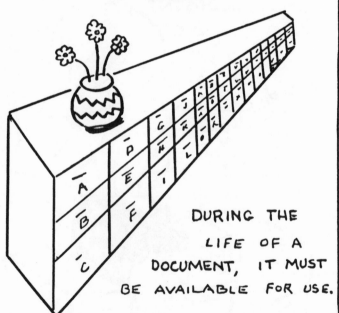

DURING THE
LIFE OF A
DOCUMENT, IT MUST
BE AVAILABLE FOR USE.

FILING SYSTEMS
ARE THE RESULT OF
THIS NEED.

ALMOST ANY FILING SYSTEM
MAY BE USED.

- BUT THOSE WHO USE THE
SYSTEM MUST BE TRAINED.

A <u>MISFILED</u>
DOCUMENT MAY BE
A <u>LOST</u> DOCUMENT.

B. GOOD MANAGEMENT
REQUIRES
ADEQUATE STORAGE.

RECORDS OF HIGH USAGE SHOULD BE STORED FOR EASY REFERENCE.

OTHERS MAY BE RELEGATED TO THE BACK ROOM OR OTHER STORAGE AREA.

GOAL 3. PROPER DISPOSITION OF RECORDS.

A. GOOD MANAGEMENT REQUIRES SYSTEMATIC DISPOSAL.

A DISPOSITION SCHEDULE GOVERNS THE RETENTION OR DISPOSITION OF RECORDS.

DISPOSITION SCHEDULE

Consumer Complaints	Destroy 1 mo. after complaint answered
Bills of Lading	Destroy 12 mo. after received
Documents Of Incorporation	PERMANENT
Company Regulations	Master copy is PERMANENT

B. GOOD MANAGEMENT
REQUIRES
SELECTIVE PRESERVATION.

RECORDS WHICH
HAVE PERMANENT VALUE
SHOULD BE IDENTIFIED AND
PRESERVED.

THOSE WHICH DON'T
SHOULD BE DESTROYED AS SOON AS
THEIR USEFULNESS ENDS.

REVIEW

Q. WHAT ARE THE GOALS
OF RECORDS MANAGEMENT ?

1. CONTROLLED_____ OF
   RECORDS.
   A. ADEQUATE_____.
   B. PREVENTION OF
      _____ DOCUMENTATION.

2. EFFICIENT_____
   OF RECORDS.
   A. _____ ARRANGEMENT
      OF FILES.
   B. ADEQUATE_____.

3. PROPER _____
   OF RECORDS.
   A. SYSTEMATIC_____
      OF RECORDS.
   B. _____ OF
      PERMANENTLY VALUABLE
      RECORDS.

CORRECT ANSWERS ARE ON PAGE 25.

CHAPTER 4
APPRAISAL of RECORDS

IN SIMPLEST TERMS,

APPRAISAL

IS DECIDING WHAT TO

KEEP AND WHAT TO

THROW AWAY.

AN ARCHIVIST MIGHT SAY :

APPRAISAL IS
DETERMINING THE VALUE
AND THUS THE
DISPOSITION OF RECORDS.

TO HELP YOU REMEMBER

1. APPRAISAL IS DETERMINING
   THE V_____ AND THUS
   THE D_____ OF RECORDS.

2. APPRAISAL IS D_____
   THE V_____ AND THUS
   THE D_____ OF R_____.

3. APPRAISAL IS D_____
   THE _____ AND THUS
   THE _____ OF_____.

SOME
WANT TO DISPOSE OF
ALMOST EVERYTHING.

IN CONTRAST TO THESE VIEWS, LET'S CONSIDER ARCHIVAL VALUE.

AN ARCHIVIST COULD DECIDE WHICH RECORDS TO RETAIN BY GUESSING.

OR,

HE COULD ASK HIMSELF
THESE
THREE QUESTIONS.

1. ARE THE RECORDS
UNIQUE ?

2. ARE THE RECORDS
USABLE ?

3. ARE THE RECORDS
REALLY
IMPORTANT ?

1. ARE THE RECORDS UNIQUE?

A UNIQUE RECORD IS A ONE-OF-A-KIND DOCUMENT.

INSTEAD OF ONE

OF MANY

IDENTICAL COPIES.

2. ARE THE RECORDS USABLE ?

A USABLE RECORD MUST MAKE INFORMATION AVAILABLE TO THE RESEARCHER.

EXAMPLES OF RECORDS WHICH ARE NOT USABLE ARE:

✓ RECORDS BADLY DAMAGED BY INSECTS, RODENTS, FIRE OR WATER.

✓ ILLEGIBLE SHORTHAND NOTES.

✓ MACHINE READABLE RECORDS IF A READER IS NO LONGER AVAILABLE,
   SUCH AS
   A. DICTAPHONE CYLINDERS,
   B. WIRE RECORDINGS, AND
   C. EARLY PHONOGRAPH RECORDINGS.

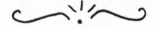

3. ARE THE RECORDS IMPORTANT ?

FIVE STANDARDS TO HELP YOU DETERMINE THE IMPORTANCE OF RECORDS.

AGE
SHOULD BE
RESPECTED.

OLDER DOCUMENTS NEED
CAREFUL CONSIDERATION
BECAUSE THEY ARE SCARCE.
HOWEVER, ALL OLD RECORDS
MAY NOT WARRANT
RETENTION.

DOCUMENTS REFLECTING PAST SUCCESSES OR FAILURES CREATE A STOREHOUSE OF EXPERIENCE.

RECORDS WHICH HAVE **VALUE** BEYOND THE **PURPOSE** FOR WHICH THEY WERE CREATED MAY NEED TO BE **RETAINED.**

HERE LIES

H. SMITH

1826 – 1908

SON OF ᵢᵣₗₙ

HUSBAND OF
ᵥₙ ᵧᵤ⁻⁻

CHILDREN:

CONT. ON BACK!

DOCUMENTS

REFLECTING THE

* ORIGIN

* ORGANIZATIONAL
    DEVELOPMENT

* PROGRAMS

* POLICIES, AND

* PROCEDURES

OF AN INSTITUTION
SHOULD BE
RETAINED
PERMANENTLY.

RECORDS ABOUT IMPORTANT PEOPLE, PLACES, EVENTS AND THINGS MAY BE KEPT PERMANENTLY.

WE HAVE CONSIDERED HOW TO
DETERMINE THE VALUE
OF RECORDS.

AND NOW...
LET'S CONSIDER

DISPOSAL OF RECORDS.

THREE GOOD REASONS

FOR DISPOSAL OF RECORDS ARE:

1. IT IS IMPOSSIBLE TO STORE ALL.

2. RESEARCH IS MADE EASIER BY GETTING RID OF TRIVIA.

3. SOME RECORDS REALLY ARE JUNK!

1. IT MAY BE
IMPOSSIBLE
TO STORE
EVERYTHING !

FIDO HAS OUTGROWN HIS DOG-HOUSE AND HE'S ONLY A PUP.

(IT COSTS APPROXIMATELY $8 PER CUBIC FOOT TO STORE RECORDS FOR ONE YEAR.)

3. SOME RECORDS REALLY ARE JUNK.

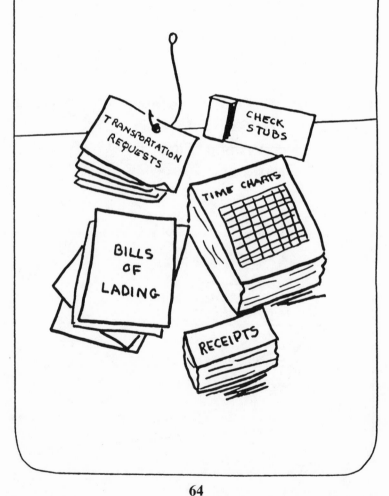

WHAT IF YOU CAN'T DECIDE ABOUT DISPOSAL?

1. KEEP THE DOCUMENTS UNTIL YOU HAVE MORE INFORMATION.

2. KEEP STATISTICAL OR SPECIAL SAMPLES. EXAMPLE:
   1 OF 100
   A'S AND B'S
   JAN. RECORDS

3. OFFER THE RECORDS TO A MUSEUM, UNIVERSITY, OR MANUSCRIPT COLLECTION.

ACCEPT

    THE FACT THAT

YOU MAY GET CRITICISM

   FOR DISPOSAL.

SO—

    CALL 'EM TOUGH

AND WALK AWAY FAST!

LET'S REVIEW

Q. IN DETERMINING THE VALUE
   OF RECORDS, WHAT THREE
   QUESTIONS MUST BE ASKED ?

1. ARE THE RECORDS

   U_____?

2. ARE THE RECORDS

   U_____?

3. ARE THE RECORDS

   I_____?

Q. WHAT ARE THREE REASONS FOR DISPOSAL OF RECORDS ?

1. IT IS _____ TO STORE ALL RECORDS.

2. RESEARCH IS MADE EASIER BY DISCARDING _____ .

3. SOME RECORDS REALLY ARE _____ .

1. IMPOSSIBLE   2. TRIVIA   3. JUNK

Chapter 5
ARRANGEMENT of ARCHIVES

THE DIFFERENCE
BETWEEN A PILE OF
ROUGH LOGS...

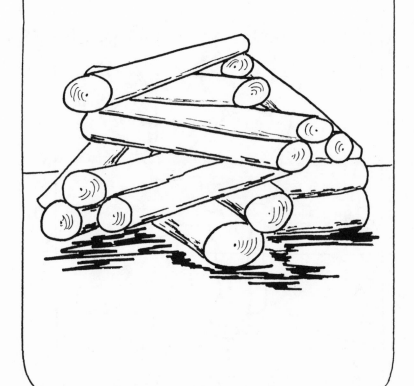

... AND A PICTURESQUE LOG CABIN IS

ARRANGEMENT.

LIKEWISE,

THE DIFFERENCE BETWEEN

A MOUNTAIN OF

PAPERS . . .

AND AN ARCHIVES

IS

ARRANGEMENT.

THE ARRANGEMENT OF RECORDS IN AN ARCHIVES MUST BE CONSIDERED ON SEVERAL LEVELS.

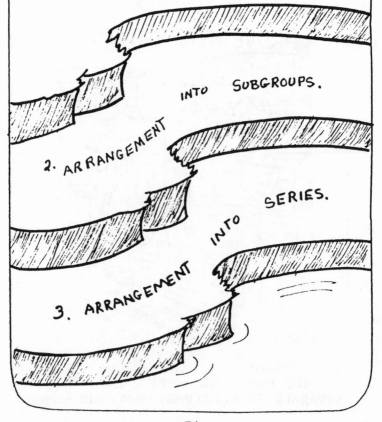

1. ARRANGEMENT ACCORDING TO ORIGIN OR PROVENANCE.

2. ARRANGEMENT INTO SUBGROUPS.

3. ARRANGEMENT INTO SERIES.

I. ARRANGEMENT ACCORDING TO
ORIGIN.

EARLY FRENCH ARCHIVISTS CALLED THIS PRINCIPLE **RESPECT** <u>des</u> **FONDS**.

PRUSSIAN ARCHIVISTS CALLED IT <u>**PROVENIENZPRINZIP**</u>.

WE CALL IT ARRANGEMENT ACCORDING TO ORIGIN or PROVENANCE.

THIS MEANS RECORDS FROM ONE SOURCE MUST BE KEPT INTACT OR SEPARATE FROM RECORDS FROM OTHER SOURCES.

FOR EXAMPLE,

IN A UNIVERSITY, RECORDS OF THE COLLEGE OF FINE ARTS MUST BE KEPT SEPARATE FROM RECORDS OF THE COLLEGE OF BUSINESS.

IN A CITY GOVERNMENT, RECORDS OF TAXATION MUST NOT BE INTERFILED WITH RECORDS OF FEDERAL GRANTS.

2. ARRANGEMENT INTO
SUBGROUPS.

IF THERE ARE MANY
RECORDS FROM A
SINGLE SOURCE,

THEY SHOULD BE
DIVIDED INTO
SUBGROUPS
REPRESENTING THE ORGANIZATION
PATTERN OF THE SOURCE.

FOR EXAMPLE,

A COLLECTION
FROM THE RESEARCH AND
DEVELOPMENT DIVISION MIGHT BE
DIVIDED INTO DEPARTMENTS OF

- ENVIRONMENTAL RESEARCH,

- MEDICAL RESEARCH, AND

- AGRICULTURAL RESEARCH

TO REFLECT THE DEPARTMENT
WHICH CREATED THE RECORDS.

ARRANGEMENT

WOULD BE EASIER _IF_...

EACH GROUP OF RECORDS
ARRIVED WITH AN
ORGANIZATION CHART.

3. ARRANGEMENT INTO SERIES.

WITHIN A SUBGROUP, ARCHIVISTS USUALLY ARRANGE RECORDS BY SERIES.

DON'T KEEP ME GUESSING. WHAT IS A SERIES ?

A SERIES IS
A GROUP OF RECORDS
RELATED BY
SUBJECT,
FUNCTION,
ACTIVITY, OR
FORM.

I KNOW THIS IS A
SERIES
BECAUSE IT IS
ALL CORRESPONDENCE
FROM THE DEAN'S
OFFICE RELATING
TO ADMISSIONS.

EXAMPLES OF SERIES ...

RELATED BY
SUBJECT :   CHEMICAL RESEARCH FILES

PROGRAM PLANNING FILES

RELATED BY
FUNCTION :   ADMISSION PROCEDURES

BAPTISMAL POLICIES

RELATED BY
ACTIVITY :   PERSONNEL FOLDERS

FUND RAISING ACTIVITIES

FISCAL RECORDS

RELATED BY
FORM :   MAPS

BLUEPRINTS

PHOTOGRAPHS

WITHIN A SERIES

RECORDS ARE ARRANGED

ACCORDING TO A

FILING SYSTEM.

AND SPEAKING
OF FILING...

THE MOST FREQUENTLY
USED
FILING SYSTEMS
ARE

CHRONOLOGICAL,

GEOGRAPHICAL,

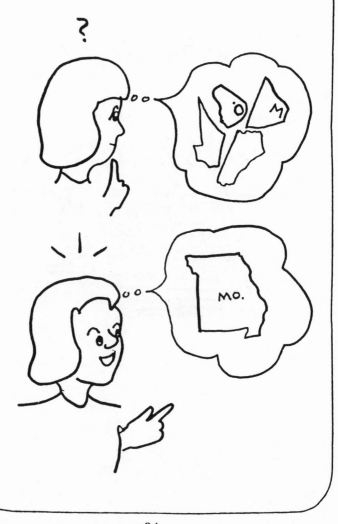

ALPHABETICAL,

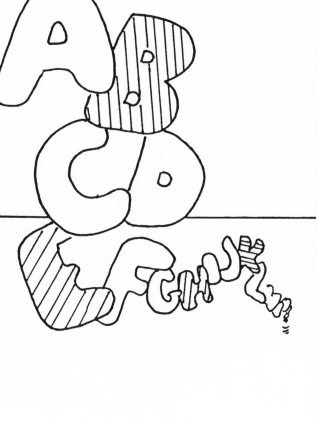

NUMERICAL,

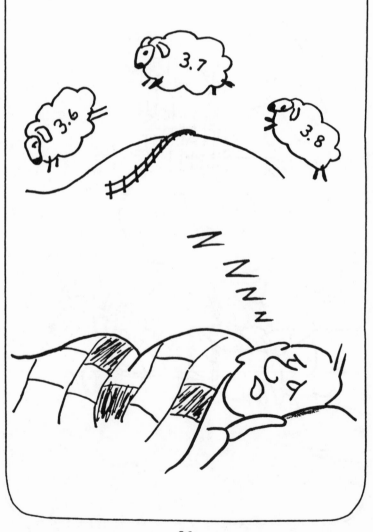

AND BY SUBJECT.

'THE TIME HAS COME,' THE
WALRUS SAID,
'TO TALK OF MANY THINGS:
OF (SHOES), AND (SHIPS),
AND (SEALING WAX),
OF (CABBAGES) AND (KINGS.)'

MOST ARCHIVISTS AGREE —

RECORDS SHOULD BE KEPT IN THEIR ORIGINAL ORDER.

THE ORGANIZATION

WHICH CREATED

THE RECORDS

ALSO CREATED

THE

ORIGINAL
ORDER .

KEEPING RECORDS
IN THEIR

ORIGINAL ORDER
PROVIDES EVIDENCES
OF THE
FUNCTION
AND
ORGANIZATION
SCHEME

OF THE
UNIT
WHICH
CREATED
THEM.

ARRANGING RECORDS

IN THEIR

ORIGINAL ORDER

USUALLY PROCEEDS
SMOOTHLY WHEN THE
PREDEVELOPED
PATTERN IS
DISCOVERED.

THE ARCHIVIST ANSWERS!

" 1. A SUBJECT HEADING CANNOT BE ALL-INCLUSIVE.

2. A SUBJECT HEADING MAY NOT ARISE FROM THE CONTENT OF A COLLECTION, FORCING IT INTO AN 'ALIEN MOLD.'

3. ONE DOCUMENT MAY DEAL WITH MANY DIFFERENT SUBJECTS, CAUSING FILING DIFFICULTIES.*

4. THE NEEDS OF RESEARCHERS CHANGE, MAKING IT DIF-FICULT TO ANTICIPATE WHICH SUBJECTS TO USE.

5. THROUGH CHANGING YEARS ORIGINAL ORDER BEST SERVES RESEARCH NEEDS. "

* SOME ARCHIVES USE CROSS-INDEXING TO AID RESEARCHERS.

ANOTHER REVIEW

1. ARCHIVAL MATERIALS SHOULD BE ARRANGED ACCORDING TO O_____ OR PROVENANCE.

2. A SERIES IS A GROUP OF RECORDS RELATED BY S_____, E_____, A_____, OR F_____.

3. MOST ARCHIVISTS ARRANGE RECORDS INTO THEIR O_____ ORDER.

CHAPTER 6
DESCRIPTION of ARCHIVES

ARRANGEMENT AND DESCRIPTION MUST GO HAND IN HAND.

ARRANGEMENT

DESCRIPTION

ARRANGING AND DESCRIBING ARCHIVES CONCURRENTLY PREVENTS NEEDLESS BACKTRACKING.

A COMPLETED
            DESCRIPTION

OF A MAJOR GROUP OF RECORDS
    IS CALLED A GUIDE
      OR AN INVENTORY.

THE GUIDE CONTAINS A (BRIEF) ADMINISTRATIVE HISTORY OF THE ORGANIZATION WHICH CREATED THE RECORDS.

HISTORY

IN THE BEGINNING GOD CREATED THE

AN ADMINISTRATIVE HISTORY TELLS THE WHO, WHERE, WHEN, AND HOW OF AN ORGANIZATION.

IN ADDITION TO THE
ADMINISTRATIVE HISTORY,

THE GUIDE
PROVIDES AN

INDEX
TO THE RECORDS DESCRIPTIONS.

IN ADDITION TO THE
ADMINISTRATIVE HISTORY AND
AN INDEX TO THE RECORDS,

THE GUIDE
ALSO PROVIDES
SERIES DESCRIPTIONS.

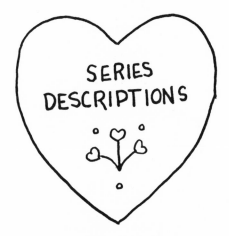

ARE THE
HEART
OF EVERY
RECORDS GUIDE.

A

SERIES DESCRIPTION

USUALLY CONTAINS
FIVE PARTS.

I. TITLE
II. DATE
III. VOLUME
IV. ARRANGEMENT
STATEMENT
V. NARRATIVE
PARAGRAPH.

PART I — SERIES DESCRIPTIONS

I. TITLE

A TITLE SHOULD BE CLEAR, DESCRIPTIVE, AND CONCISE. IT WILL USUALLY CONTAIN THE FOLLOWING ELEMENTS.

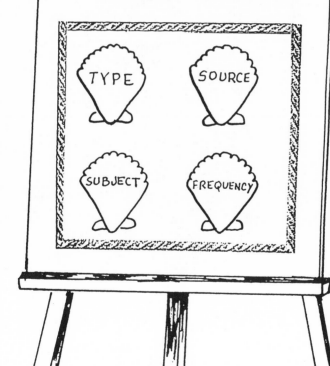

TYPE   SOURCE

SUBJECT   FREQUENCY

TYPE

THE TITLE OF A
SERIES WILL IDENTIFY
THE SPECIFIC
TYPE OR KIND OF
RECORD BEING DESCRIBED.

SPECIFIC TERMS ARE PREFERRED
TO GENERAL TERMS, SUCH AS
PAPERS, RECORDS, OR DOCUMENTS.

A FEW OF THE MANY TYPES OF RECORDS ARE:

ARTWORK
APPLICATIONS
BLUEPRINTS
CONTRACTS
CORRESPONDENCE
DIRECTIVES
DESPATCHES
DAYBOOKS
GUIDES
JOURNALS
LETTERPRESS
      COPYBOOKS
MAPS
ORDERS
PHOTOGRAPHS
QUESTIONNAIRES
READING FILES
REPORTS
ROLLS

THE TITLE WILL ALSO INDICATE THE **SOURCE** OR **CREATOR** OF THE DOCUMENTS.

THE SOURCE MAY BE VERY IMPORTANT.

SARGE SIGNED THIS! I'LL READ IT AGAIN... AND AGAIN...

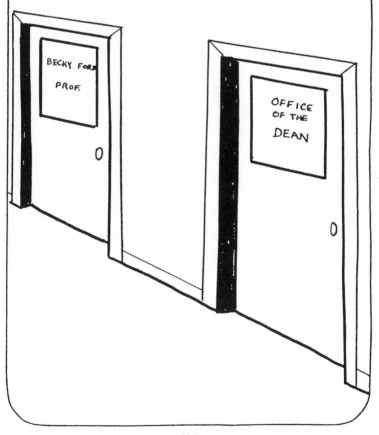

THE SOURCE OF A SERIES OF RECORDS MIGHT BE AN INDIVIDUAL, OR AN OFFICE.

THE TITLE
WILL INDICATE THE
SUBJECT
OF THE SERIES, IF
POSSIBLE.

SOME SERIES, SUCH AS CORRESPONDENCE, INCLUDE MORE THAN ONE SUBJECT.

IN THIS CASE, THE FUNCTION OR THE ACTIVITY OF THE SERIES MAY BECOME THE SUBJECT.

I BELIEVE THE SUBJECT OF THIS SERIES SHOULD BE FINANCIAL REPORTS.

REPORTS OF THE TREASURER

IN ADDITION, THE TITLE WILL STATE THE **FREQUENCY** OF THE CREATION OF THE RECORDS.

I WRITE SALLY EVERY DAY! HOW OFTEN DO I WRITE MY MOTHER?

MONTHLY.

LOOK AT THESE EXAMPLES OF TITLES :

1. Weekly Child Care Bulletins from Becky Ford.
2. Treasurer's Monthly Financial Reports.

NOW IT'S YOUR TURN. COMPOSE THREE SERIES TITLES BY CHOOSING ELEMENTS FROM THE LISTS BELOW.

TYPE	SOURCE	SUBJECT	FREQUENCY
minutes	president	railroads	daily
reports	biologist	legal	weekly
letters	pastor	wild cats	monthly
dockets	composer	baptism	annually
sermons	personnel	salaries	each spring
telegrams	committee	marriage	final
ballads	engineer	financial	occasional

1. _____

_____

2. _____

_____

3. _____

_____

II. DATE

FOLLOWING THE TITLE, STATE THE DATE OF THE SERIES.

Indicate exact, inclusive dates when possible. For example, (1890–1920). If a gap occurs in the records from 1911 to 1914, write as follows (1890–1910; 1915–1920).

If a few items are dated before or after the main body of records, state this in the narrative description.

PART III - SERIES DESCRIPTIONS

III. VOLUME

AFTER THE TITLE
AND THE DATE
INDICATE THE

QUANTITY

OF RECORDS
IN TERMS OF FEET
OR INCHES.

IF RECORDS ARE
BOUND, GIVE NUMBER
OF VOLUMES.

FOR EXAMPLE,

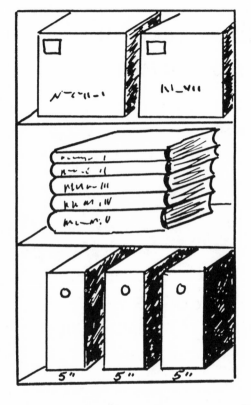

2 FT.

5 B.V.

15 IN.

A CARTON MEASURING 12" x 15" x 10"
IS COUNTED AS ONE FOOT OF RECORDS.

BOUND VOLUME IS ABBREVIATED B.V.

AN ARCHIVES BOX IS ABOUT
   5" WIDE.

IV. ARRANGEMENT STATEMENT.

Many times it is helpful to include an arrangement statement in the description.* Remember, the most used arrangements are chronological, geographical, alphabetical, numerical, and by subject.

> *Ex.* Arranged alphabetically by surname of individual.

> *Ex.* Arranged geographically by state and thereunder by county.

*Some archivists prefer to place the arrangement statement after the narrative paragraph.

Ⅴ. NARRATIVE PARAGRAPH.

A narrative paragraph presents additional information about
* the substance of the records,
* the creator of the records,
* the dates,
* the relationship to other records.

Here is an example:
Administrative files of George Parks relating to the organization of the Ouray County Library. Included are correspondence, blueprints, lists of donors, and photographs. Most of the files are dated 1890–1907, although miscellaneous items are dated as late as 1923. For related records see Financial Files, Ouray County.

NOW,
LET'S EXAMINE A COMPLETE SERIES DESCRIPTION.

TITLE DATE VOLUME

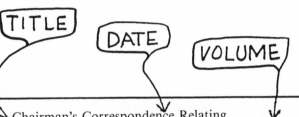

Chairman's Correspondence Relating to Railroads. 1887–1896. 9 ft. 8 b.v.

Arranged chronologically.

Letters received and copies of letters sent relating to the construction and operation of the Fort Worth-Denver Railroad. A few newspaper clippings are included. The "letters sent" are in press-copy volumes. The final three letters are dated 1902. For related records, see Railroad Land Grants, 1880–1893.

ARRANGEMENT STATEMENT

NARRATIVE PARAGRAPH

REVIEW

1. A RECORDS GUIDE OR INVENTORY INCLUDES AN I_____, AN ADMINISTRATIVE H_____, AND S_____ D_____.

2. THE FIVE PARTS OF A COMPLETE SERIES DESCRIPTION ARE T_____, D_____, V_____, A_____ S_____, AND N_____ P_____.

3. A TITLE WILL INDICATE T_____ OF RECORD, S_____, S_____ AND F_____ OF CREATION.

1. INDEX, HISTORY, SERIES DESCRIPTIONS. 2. TITLE, DATE, VOLUME, ARRANGEMENT STATEMENT, NARRATIVE PARAGRAPH. 3. TYPE, SOURCE, SUBJECT, FREQUENCY.

116

CHAPTER 7
PRESERVATION of ARCHIVES

PRESERVATION

MEANS DIFFERENT
THINGS TO DIFFERENT
PEOPLE.

TO A CHEF
IT MEANS MAKING PICKLES.

TO A
LADY,

PRESERVATION MEANS
PREVENTING
WRINKLES.

TO AN ARCHIVIST, PRESERVATION MEANS PREVENTING THE DETERIORATION OF ARCHIVAL MATERIAL.

SOME OF THE FORCES

WHICH DAMAGE
DOCUMENTS ARE:

{ HEAT
  HUMIDITY
  LIGHT
  FIRE
  FLOOD

{ RODENTS
  INSECTS

{ THEFT
  MUTILATION

TO HELP YOU REMEMBER:

✓ THE FIRST <u>FIVE</u> CAUSES
  ARE NATURAL.

✓ THE NEXT <u>TWO</u> ARE ANIMAL.

✓ THE LAST <u>TWO</u> ARE HUMAN.

RECORDS DAMAGE
OCCURS BOTH
INTERNALLY AT THE
DOCUMENT LEVEL
AND EXTERNALLY IN
THE STORAGE FACILITY.

ADEQUATE PROCESSING
FOR PRESERVATION AT
THE DOCUMENT LEVEL
INCLUDES
- CLEANING,
- REMOVING EXTRANEOUS
  MATERIAL,
- FLATTENING,
- DEACIDIFYING, AND
- STORING IN ACID-FREE
  CONTAINERS.

AN ADEQUATE
ARCHIVAL STORAGE AREA
PROVIDES

SAFETY

IN MANY WAYS.

FOR AN EXAMPLE
PLEASE
TURN PAGE

GOOB
RULE BERG'S
IDEAL
ARCHIVES

1. LOW-LEVEL LIGHTING
2. FIRE CONTROL
3. INSECT CONTROL
4. HUMIDITY CONTROL
5. RODENT REGULATOR
6. ACID-FREE CONTAINERS
7. TEMPERATURE REGULATOR
8. FLOOD CONTROL
9. THEFT PREVENTION

WELL, YES !

MR. RULEBERG HAS THE
RIGHT IDEA,

EVEN THOUGH
SOME OF HIS
METHODS
ARE A LITTLE
UNSOPHISTICATED.

 AND HERE
IS A BASIC
RULE of THUMB
FOR
PRESERVATIONISTS
—

IF ARCHIVES BUDGET IS LIMITED, CONCENTRATE ON PRESERVING

THE MAJORITY OF RECORDS THROUGH PROPER STORAGE, RATHER THAN EXPENDING INTENSIVE TREATMENT ON INDIVIDUAL DOCUMENTS.

———

LET'S REVIEW

1. SOME DESTRUCTIVE FORCES
   WHICH MAY DAMAGE
   ARCHIVAL MATERIALS ARE

   _____ ⎫
   _____ ⎬ NATURAL
   _____ ⎭ CAUSES
   _____

   _____ ⎫ ANIMAL
   _____ ⎬ CAUSES

   _____ ⎫ HUMAN
   _____ ⎬ CAUSES

2. DAMAGE AT THE DOCUMENT
   LEVEL MAY BE PREVENTED
   BY C_____,
   R_____ E_____ M_____,
   F_____,
   D_____, AND
   S_____ IN A____-F_____
   CONTAINERS.

128

Chapter 8
Reference Service

TO MAKE THE RECORDS

AVAILABLE

TO THOSE WHO NEED THEM.

A

THAT'S THE BOTTOM LINE.

ARCHIVISTS CALL THIS
REFERENCE SERVICE.

REFERENCE SERVICE AIDS
THE PUBLIC IN FIVE WAYS.

1. INFORMATION SERVICE.
2. PHYSICAL SERVICE.
3. DOCUMENT SERVICE.
4. EXHIBITS.
5. PUBLICATIONS.

I. INFORMATION SERVICE.

MR. JOE DOUGH TELEPHONES THE ARCHIVIST. "WHEN WAS FLORIDA STATE UNIVERSITY ESTABLISHED?" HE ASKS.

THE ARCHIVIST MAY LOOK IN THE RECORDS AND GIVE AN IMMEDIATE REPLY.

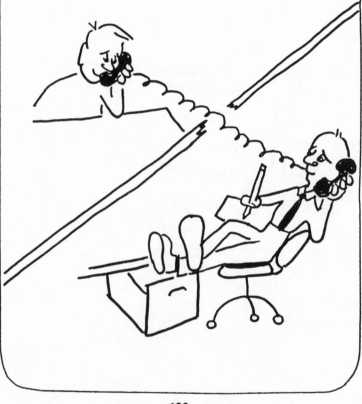

OR, IF THE ANSWER REQUIRES EXTENSIVE RESEARCH, THE ARCHIVIST MAY SEND A DESCRIPTION OF THE RECORDS WHERE THE INFORMATION MAY BE FOUND.

2. PHYSICAL SERVICE.

JOE DOUGH, MRS. DOUGH, AND FIVE SMALL BISCUITS COME TO THE ARCHIVES REQUESTING TO SEE THE RECORDS OF THE INSTITUTION.

HOW SHOULD THEIR REQUEST BE HANDLED?

THE ARCHIVIST WILL
PROVIDE FINDING AIDS TO THE
RESEARCHER. HE WILL
POINT OUT INSTITUTIONAL RULES
AND ASK FOR COMPLIANCE.

THE RULES MIGHT INCLUDE:

HOURS OF SERVICE,
IDENTIFICATION REQUIREMENTS,
AGE RESTRICTIONS,
SECURITY REQUIREMENTS,
EATING, SMOKING
RESTRICTIONS.

3. DOCUMENT SERVICE.

AN ARCHIVES MAY
LOAN RECORDS

OR
PROVIDE AUTHENTICATED
COPIES.

4. EXHIBIT SERVICE.

AN INSTITUTION MAY
REQUEST AN EXHIBIT
TO CELEBRATE

A MILESTONE IN
INSTITUTIONAL LIFE

OR TO ACQUAINT THE PUBLIC WITH ARCHIVAL HOLDINGS.

RULES FOR PRESERVATION MUST BE OBSERVED DURING AN EXHIBIT. PROTECT THE MATERIALS FROM THEFT, MUTILATION, DIRECT SUNLIGHT, ETC.

5. PUBLICATIONS.

IN ADDITION TO
PUBLISHED DESCRIPTIONS
OF
RECORDS GROUPS,
AN ARCHIVES MAY CHOOSE
TO MICROFILM
IMPORTANT SERIES OF PAPERS.

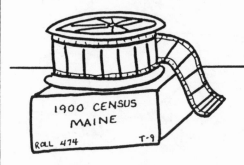

MICROFILM PROTECTS ORIGINAL RECORDS BY TAKING THEM FROM CIRCULATION.

MICROFILM MAY BE EASILY COPIED FOR RESEACHERS IN DISTANT LOCATIONS.

REVIEW

FIVE ACTIVITIES OF REFERENCE SERVICE ARE:

1. _____

2. _____

3. _____

4. _____

5. _____

1. INFORMATION SERVICE.   2. PHYSICAL SERVICE.
3. DOCUMENT SERVICE.   4. EXHIBITS.   5. PUBLICATIONS.

141

SUMMARY

Chapter 1: What Are Archives?

Are archives places where historical documents are kept?

That's right! Archives are places or institutions where non-current records are stored.

But, they are more than places. Archives are also certain kinds of records. Sir Hilary Jenkinson, an English archivist, said, "Archives are documents drawn up in an official transaction and preserved for information."

Note the three main words in Jenkinson's definition.

1. Documents.
2. Official.
3. Preserved.

1. Archives are documents. Documents can be made of paper, wood, stone, tape, or any other material which can carry a message.

2. Archives are official. They were created to keep account of transactions in the regular course of business.

3. Archives are permanently preserved.

By the way, here's another important fact about archives. Archives are usually the official records of a single institution. Some archives include special collections, such as personal papers or manuscripts.

Generally, an archives collects only the permanent records of a parent institution.

For example, the Louisiana State Archives accepts only records from the Louisiana State Government — not from Oregon, Ohio, nor Texas.

Southern Baptist Seminary does not collect records from Notre Dame University.

The National Archives collects only records created by Federal agencies.

Chapter 2: Why Do We Need Archives?

Here are six reasons we need archives:

1. Archives preserve primary sources. Unlike history books or newspapers, archives are unbiased by the viewpoint of author or journalist.

2. Archives make efficient research possible. In an archival repository, a researcher can have a lot of information at his fingertips.

3. Archives preserve our cultural heritage.

4. Archives fill an official need.

5. Archives protect the public interest.

6. Archives free office space for current operations.

Chapter 3: Records Management

Why should an archivist care about records management? Because both archivists and records managers are concerned with the whole life span of records: creation, management, and disposition.

What are the goals of a records manager? They are almost the same as the goals of an archivist.

The goals of records management are:

1. Controlled creation of records.
   A. Adequate documentation.
   B. Prevention of unnecessary documentation.
2. Efficient management of records.
   A. Efficient arrangement of files.
   B. Adequate storage.
3. Proper disposition of records.
   A. Systematic disposal.
   B. Preservation of permanently valuable records.

Let's look at these goals one by one.

1. Controlled creation of records.
   A. Good management requires adequate documentation. The most valuable records of an organization relate to

origin, developments, and major programs. Such records should be preserved.

B. Good management requires prevention of unnecessary documentation.

With the development of the typewriter, paperwork began to increase. Later, carbon paper made multiple copies possible. Photocopiers multiplied the production and the problem. Of course, administrators want many reports. However, the cry of the records manager is "simplify, simplify, simplify."

2. Efficient management of records.

A. Good management requires efficient arrangement of files.

During the life of a document, it must be available for use. Filing systems are the result of this need. Almost any filing system may be used, but those who use the system must be trained.

B. Good management requires adequate storage.

Records of high usage should be stored for easy reference. Others may be relegated to the back room. Wherever they are stored, records need to be accessible and secure.

3. Proper disposition of records.

A. Good management requires systematic disposal.

A disposition schedule governs the retention or disposition of records.

B. Good management requires selective preservation.

Records which may be permanent value should be identified and preserved. Those which don't should be destroyed as soon as their usefulness ends.

Chapter 4: Appraisal of Records

In simplest terms, appraisal is deciding what to keep and what to throw away. An archivist might say, "Appraisal is determining the value and thus the disposition of records."

Archivists see appraisal from many different viewpoints. Some want to dispose of almost everything. Some want to keep it all. In contrast to these views, let us consider archival value.

An archivist could decide which records to retain by guessing. Or, he could ask himself three questions:

1. Are the records unique?

A unique record is a one-of-a-kind document instead of one of many identical copies.

2. Are the records usable?

A usable record must make information available to the researcher. Examples of records which are not usable are:

- records badly damaged by insects, rodents, fire or water,
- illegible shorthand notes, or
- machine readable records if a reader is no longer available.

3. Are the records important?

There are five standards to help you determine the importance of records:

A. Age should be respected.

Older documents need careful consideration because they are scarce. However, all old records may not warrant retention.

B. Documents reflecting past successes or failures create a storehouse of experience.

C. Records which have value beyond the purpose for which they were created may need to be retained.

D. Documents reflecting the origin, organizational development, programs, policies and procedures of an institution should be retained permanently.

We have considered how to determine the value of records. Now, let's consider the disposal of records. Three good reasons for disposal are:

1. It is impossible to store all records.
2. Research is made easier by discarding trivia.
3. Some records really are worthless.

What if you can't decide about disposal? Keep the documents until you have more information. Keep statistical or special samples. Or, offer the records to a museum, university or manuscript collection.

Accept the fact that you may get criticism for disposal.

Chapter 5: Arrangement of Archives

The difference between a pile of broken glass and a stained glass window is arrangement. Also, the difference between a mountain of papers and an archives is arrangement.

The arrangement of records in an archives must be considered on several levels:

1. Arrangement according to origin.

French archivists called this principle *respect des fonds*. Prussian archivists called it *provenienzprinzip*. We call it arrangement according to origin or provenance. This means that records from one source must be kept intact or separate from records from other sources. For example, in a university, records of the college of fine arts must be kept separate from records of the college of business.

2. Arrangement into subgroups.

If there are many records from a single source, they should be divided into groups representing the organization pattern of the source. For example, a collection from the research development division might be divided into the departments of environmental research, medical research, and agricultural research to reflect the department which created the records.

3. Arrangement into series.

Within a subgroup, archivists usually arrange records by series, which is a group of records related by subject, function, activity or form.

Examples of series

—related by subject:	Chemical research files
	Program planning files
—related by function:	Admission procedures
	Baptism policies
—related by activity:	Personnel folders
	Fund raising activities
—related by form:	Maps
	Blueprints
	Photographs

Most archivists agree that records should be kept in their original order. The organization which created the records also created the original order. Keeping records in their original order provides evidences of the function and organization scheme of the unit which created them. Arranging records in their original order usually proceeds smoothly when the predeveloped pattern is discovered.

The researcher asks, "Why can't archives be organized by subject?"

The archivist answers, "A subject heading cannot be all-inclusive. A subject heading may not arise from the content of a collection, forcing it into an 'alien mold.' One document may deal with many different subjects, causing filing difficulties. The needs of research change, making it difficult to anticipate which subjects to use. Through changing years, original order best serves all needs."

Chapter 6: Description of Archives

Arranging and describing archives concurrently prevents needless backtracking.

A completed description of a major group of records is called a guide or inventory. A guide contains a brief administrative history of the organization which created the records. The history tells the who, where and how of an organization.

The guide also provides an index to the records and series descriptions. Series descriptions are the heart of every records guide.

A series description usually specifies title, date, volume, arrangement and contains a narrative paragraph about the records.

I. Title.

A title should be clear, descriptive, and concise. It will usually specify the type, source, subject, and frequency of creation of the records.

Type. The title will identify the specific type or kind of record being described. Specific terms are preferred to general terms, such as papers, records or documents. A few of the many types of records are applications, contracts, correspondence, directives, despatches, daybooks, guides, journals, letterpress

148

copybooks, maps, orders, photographs, questionnaires, reading files, reports, rolls and speeches.

Source. The title will also indicate the source or creator of the documents. The source of a series of records might be an individual or an office.

Subject. The title will indicate the subject of the series, if possible. Some series, such as correspondence, include more than one subject. In this case, the function or the activity may become the subject.

Frequency. In addition, the title will state the frequency of the creation of the records.

II. Date.

Indicate exact, inclusive dates when possible. If a gap occurs in the records, write as follows (1890-1910; 1915-1920).

III. Volume.

Indicate the quantity of records in terms of feet or inches. If records are bound, give the number of volumes.

IV. Arrangement statement.

Many times it is helpful to include an arrangement statement in the description. The most used arrangements are chronological, geographical, alphabetical, numerical and by subject.

ex. Arranged alphabetically by surname of individual.

ex. Arranged geographically by state and thereunder by county.

(Some archivists prefer to place the arrangement statement after the narrative paragraph.)

V. Narrative paragraph.

A narrative paragraph presents additional information about the substance of the records, the creator of the records, the dates, the relationship to other records.

Here is an example:

Administrative files of George Parks relating to the organization of the Ouray County Library. Included are correspondence, blueprints, lists of donors and photographs. Most of the files are dated 1891-1907, although miscellaneous items are dated as late as 1923. For related records, see Financial Files, 1887-1926, Ouray County.

Now, let's examine a complete series description.

Chairman's Correspondence Relating to Railroads. (title)
1887–1896. (date)   9 ft. 8 b.v. (volume)
       Arranged chronologically. (arrangement statement)

Letters received and copies of letters sent relating to the construction and operation of the Fort Worth–Denver Railroad. A few newspaper clippings are included. The "letters sent" are in press-copy volumes. The final three letters are dated 1902. For related records, see Railroad Land Grants, 1880–1893. (narrative paragraph)

Chapter 7: Preservation of Archives

Preservation means different things to different people. To a chef, it means making pickles. To a lady, preservation means preventing wrinkles. To an archivist, preservation means preventing the deterioration of archival materials.

Some of the forces which damage documents are heat, humidity, light, fire, and flood, rodents and insects, theft and mutilation.

Records damage occurs both internally at the document level and externally in the storage facility. Adequate processing for preservation at the document level includes cleaning, removing extraneous material, flattening, deacidifying, and storing in acid-free containers.

An adequate storage facility provides safety in many ways: low-level lighting, fire control, insect control, humidity control, rodent control, acid-free containers, temperature regulation, flood control and theft prevention.

A basic rule of thumb for preservationists is: When the archives budget is limited, concentrate on preserving the majority of records through proper storage, rather than expending intensive treatment on individual documents.

Chapter 8: Reference Service

Why should we arrange, describe and preserve records in an archives? To make the records available for research. Archivists call this reference service. Reference service aids the public in five ways.

1. Information service.

Joe Dough telephones the archivist. "When was Florida State University established and who was the first president?" he asks. The archivist may look in the records and give an immediate reply. However, if the answer requires extensive research, the archivist may send a description of the records where the information may be found.

2. Physical service.

Joe Dough, Mrs. Dough and their five small children come to the archives requesting to see the records of the institution. How should their request be handled? The archivist will provide finding aids to the researcher. He will point out institutional rules and ask for compliance. The rules might include hours of service, identification requirements, age restrictions, security requirements, and eating and smoking restrictions.

3. Document service.

An archives may loan records or provide authenticated copies. Providing copies is the preferred method.

4. Exhibit service.

An institution may request an exhibit to celebrate a milestone in institutional life, or to acquaint the public with archival holdings. Rules for preservation must be observed during an exhibit. Protect the materials from theft, direct light, mutilation, and so forth.

5. Publications.

In addition to published descriptions of record groups, an archives may choose to microfilm important series of papers. Microfilm protects original records by taking them from circulation. Microfilm may be easily copied for researchers in distant locations.

BIBLIOGRAPHY

Baumann, Roland, ed. *A Manual of Archival Techniques.* Penn Hist. and Museum, 1982.

Brichford, Maynard J. *Archives and Manuscripts: Appraisal and Accessioning,* rev. ed. Society American Archivists, 1977.

Casterline, Gail F. *Archives and Manuscripts: Exhibits.* Society American Archivists, 1980.

Cunha, George M. and Cunha, Dorothy G. *Library and Archives Conservation: 1980's and Beyond.* Scarecrow, 1983.

Duchein, Michel. *Archive Buildings and Equipment.* K.G. Saur, 1977.

Ehrenberg, Ralph E. *Archives and Manuscripts: Maps and Architectual Drawings.* Society American Archivists, 1982.

Evans, Frank B. *A Basic Glossary for Archivists, Manuscript Curators, and Records Managers.* Society American Archivists, 1974.

Fleckner, John A. *Archives and Manuscripts: Surveys.* Society American Archivists, 1977.

Gracy, David B. *Archives and Manuscripts: Arrangement and Description,* rev. ed. Society American Archivists, 1977.

Gunner, Jean. *Simple Repair and Preservation Techniques for Collection Curators, Librarians, and Archivists.* Hunt Int. Botanical, 1984.

Hedstrom, Margaret L. *Archives and Manuscripts: Machine Readable Records.* Society American Archivists, 1984.

Holbert, Sue E. *Archives and Manuscripts: Reference and Accession.* Society American Archivists, 1977.

Lytle, Richard H., ed. *Management of Archives and Manuscript Collections for Librarians.* Society American Archivists, 1980.

National Research Council. *Preservation of Historical Records.* National Academy Press, 1986.

Pardo, Thomas C. *Basic Archival Workshops: A Handbook for the Workshop Organizer.* Society American Archivists, 1982.

Peterson, Trudy H. *Basic Archival Workshop Exercises.* Society American Archivists, 1982.

Ritzenthaler, Mary L., et. al. *Administration of Photographic Collections.* Society American Archivists, 1984.

_____. *Archives and Manuscripts: Conservation.* Society American Archivists, 1983.

Sandifer, Kevin W. *Religious Archives, A Complete Technical Look for the Layman.* Archival Services, 1985.

Schellenberg, T.R. *Modern Archives: Principles and Techniques.* Midway Reprint Service, University of Chicago Press, 1975.

Society American Archivists Committee of College and University Archives, ed. *College and University Archives Selected Readings.* Society American Archivists, 1979.

Sueflow, August R. *Religious Archives: An Introduction.* Society American Archivists, 1980.

Taylor, Hugh. *The Arrangement and Description of Archival Materials.* ICA Handbook Service, 1980.

Walch, Timothy. *Archives and Manuscripts: Security.* Society American Archivists, 1977.

Whalen, Lucille and Katz, Bill, eds. *Reference Service in Archives.* Haworth, 1986.